LITTLE MYTHS

HERCULES

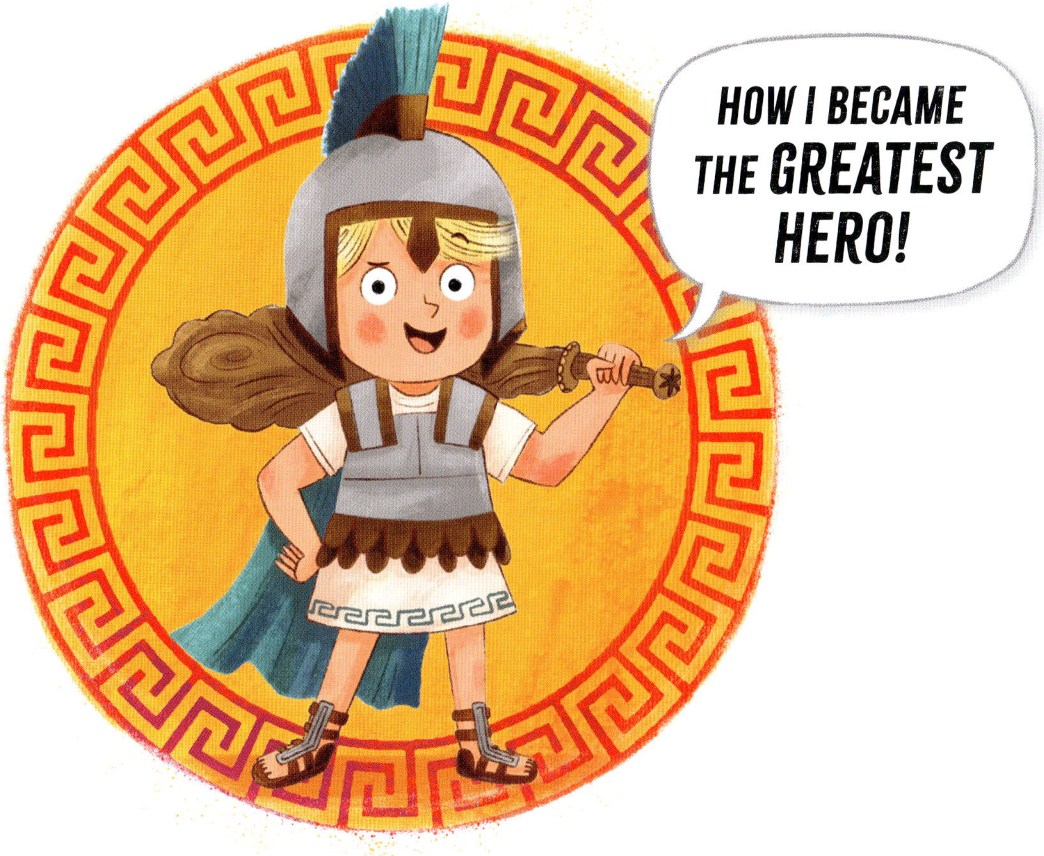
HOW I BECAME THE GREATEST HERO!

WRITTEN BY
ALEXANDRA STEWART

ILLUSTRATED BY
KATIE KEAR

HODDER

and feast your eyes on that **swishy** cape.

I know what you're thinking (apart from: 'does that cape come with matching pants and tights?')! You're thinking: 'I wouldn't want to get on this guy's bad side!'

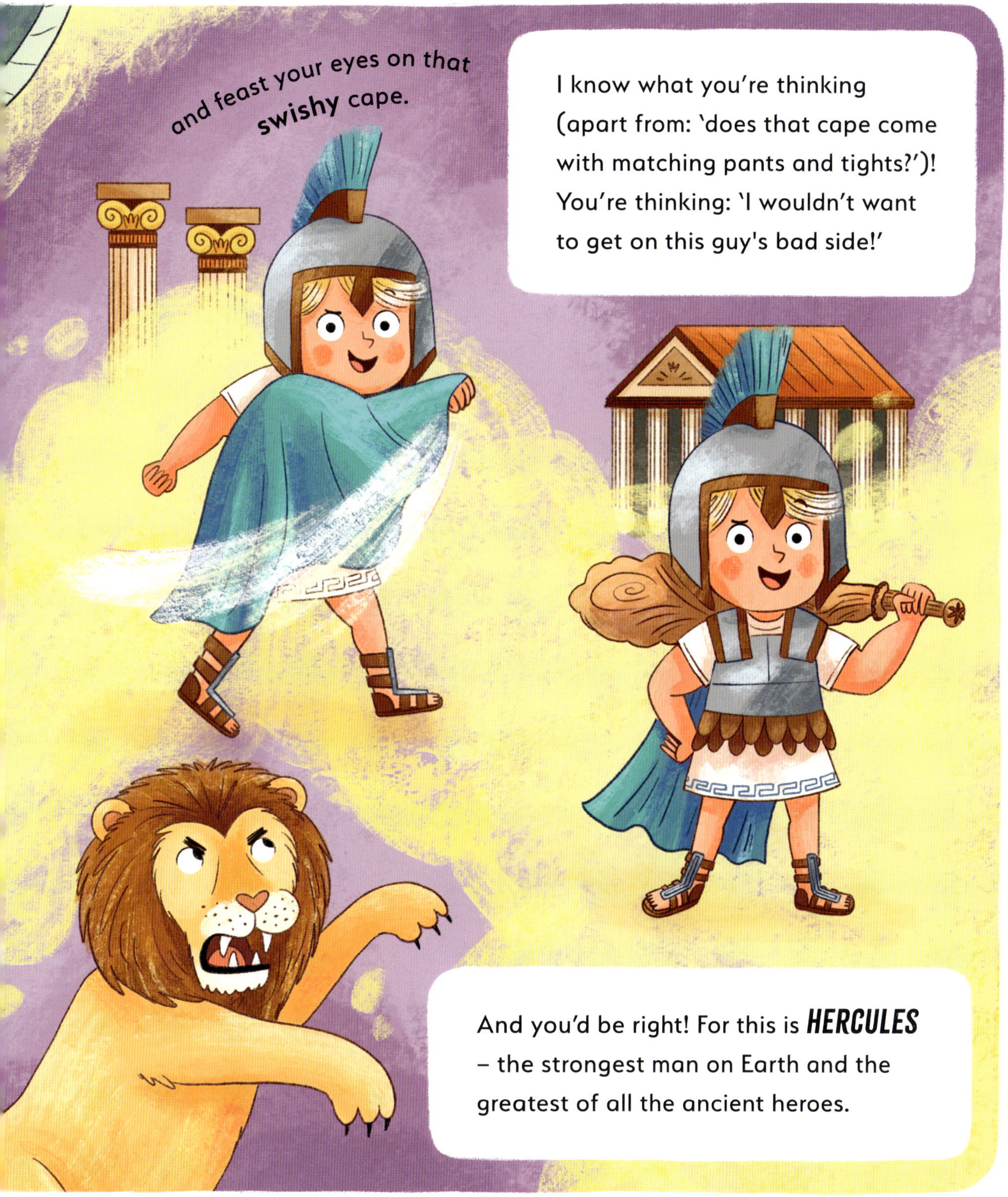

And you'd be right! For this is ***HERCULES*** – the strongest man on Earth and the greatest of all the ancient heroes.

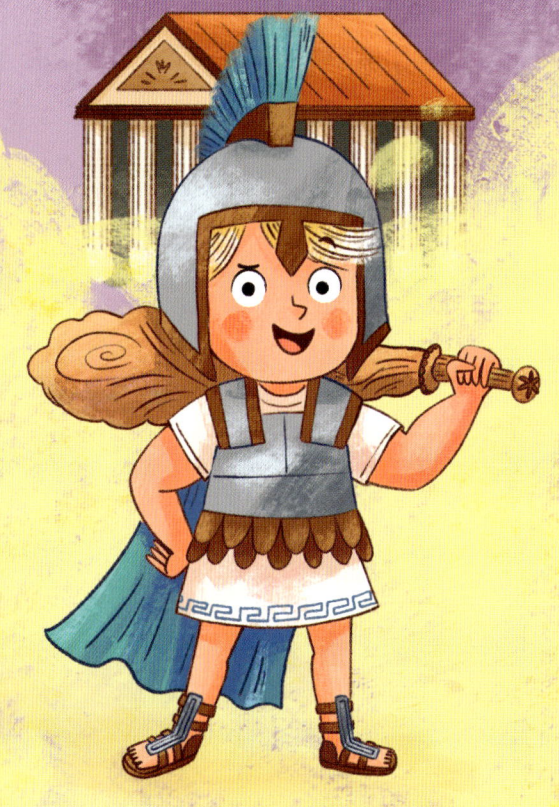

all without breaking a sweat!

He could be the very best of friends and the very worst of enemies.

Which will come as no surprise when you consider that his father was none other than the mighty ZEUS, king of the gods!

But who was Hercules's mum?

Here she is, the beautiful and wise ALCMENE, a **mortal** princess who lived with her husband, AMPHITRYON, in the city of THEBES.

Long story short: after a visit from Zeus (who had disguised himself as Amphitryon) Alcmene gave birth to twins:

Now, Alcmene knew that the fearsome goddess HERA – Zeus's waspish wife – would probably want to punish her. So, she abandoned baby Hercules!

Luckily, the goddess ATHENA scooped him up and asked Hera to feed him. Not recognising who the howling baby was, Hera agreed.

When she realised what had happened, Hera boiled with rage. That night, as Hercules slept, two slithering assassins slipped into his cradle.

"That'll sort him out," sniggered Hera.

When Alcmene awoke the next morning, she discovered . . . a happy Hercules cooing with joy. Gripped tightly in his pudgy hands were his favourite new toys: two limp and lifeless snakes.

One day, while Hercules was practising his lyre, his music teacher, Linus, tried to correct him.

EXPLODING in a fiery fit of fury, Hercules struck Linus with his lyre. CLUNK! And killed him!

Hercules clearly needed a time out. So, Amphitryon sent him far, far away to tend his animals on Mount Cithaeron.

Older, wiser and feeling ready for some heroics, he returned to Thebes just in time to save the city from an enemy attack! The King of Thebes was so delighted, he let Hercules marry his daughter, MEGARA.

Desperate to make amends for his terrible crime, Hercules asked the DELPHIC ORACLE for advice.

So, Hercules made his way to TIRYNS for a meeting with slippery KING EURYSTHEUS.

Task number one was to slay the **Nemean Lion** – a beast with skin so tough that no weapon could pierce it.

Hercules strangled the lion and cut off its skin using its own claw.

Check out my new cape!

Yeah . . . not really my vibe. But enjoy wearing it while you can. Clothes are no use to dead heroes . . . mwahaha.

Task number two was to kill the **Hydra** –
a many-headed monster with poisonous blood and breath.

Each time Hercules chopped off one of the heads, two grew back!

So, while Hercules lopped off the heads, his nephew, Iolaus, quickly burned the stumps before their replacements could grow back. Problem solved!

The tasks got harder and harder. Hercules had to:

Capture the rampaging **Cretan bull** . . .

and the man-eating horses of **King Diomedes**.

Bring back the **girdle (belt) of Hippolyta**, Queen of the Amazons.

Steal cattle from **Geryon**, the three-headed giant.

And collect the golden apples of the **Hesperides** (nymphs).

I'm actually more of Granny Smith man myself . . .

His final task was to bring **Cerberus**, the three-headed hound of HADES, up from the **underworld** (that's the world of the dead!) . . .

. . . which he did, much to Eurystheus's surprise!

All **12** tasks complete, Hercules was free to go.

Now, you might think he'd had enough of heroics . . .

Not a bit of it! Hercules went on to have many more adventures –

battling baddies,

settling old scores . . .

and fighting in the **Gigantomachy**, a massive god versus giant showdown.

He even saved Hera from the king of the giants . . .

which was pretty decent of him, all things considered.

Oh, and he got married again to the lovely PRINCESS DEIANIRA whose name means 'man destroyer'! Can you see where this is heading? Hercules had finally met his match.

It wasn't Deianira's fault, to be fair. She was tricked by a scheming centaur into giving Hercules a shirt that had been dipped in the Hydra's fatal venom.

And, if you look upwards on a clear night, you might see his figure in the stars. The fifth largest constellation – a fitting tribute to the ancient world's favourite superstar!

Hercules was worshipped by ancient Greeks and Romans.

The Romans called him **Hercules**, which is how he is more commonly known today, but the Greeks called him **Heracles**. Two names for the same hero!

The stories of Hercules were passed down from mouth-to-mouth (orally) over the centuries. They were eventually written down, by different people, in different times and in different places. For this reason, there are many different versions of the events of his life!

IMMORTAL: a being that never dies (they live forever).

MORTAL: a human being who will, one day, die.

HERO: in ancient Greek and Roman mythology, a hero was a mortal with superhuman abilities. They had these special abilities because they were descended from a god.

For the lion-hearted Crouch family! - A.S.

For Michael, who has walked every step of this journey with me. - K.K.

HODDER CHILDREN'S BOOKS
First published in Great Britain in 2026 by
Hodder and Stoughton Limited

Text and illustrations copyright © Hodder and Stoughton 2026
Text by Alexandra Stewart
Illustrations by Katie Kear

The author and illustrator hereby waive all moral rights as defined in Chapter IV of the Copyright, Designs and Patents Act 1988 and any equivalent rights in any jurisdiction to the extent that such waiver is permitted by law.

All rights reserved. A CIP catalogue record for this book is available from the British Library.

HB ISBN: 978-1-444-96962-7
E-book ISBN: 978-1-444-98028-8

1 3 5 7 9 10 8 6 4 2

Printed in China

Hodder Children's Books
An imprint of Hachette Children's Group
Part of Hodder and Stoughton Limited
Carmelite House, 50 Victoria Embankment
London EC4Y 0DZ

An Hachette UK Company
www.hachette.co.uk
www.hachettechildrens.co.uk

The authorised representative in the EEA is Hachette Ireland, 8 Castlecourt Centre, Dublin 15, D15 XTP3, Ireland (email: info@hbgi.ie)